JEST IN PUN

Sidesplitters from Bil Keane's

SBS SCHOLASTIC BOOK SERVICES
New York Toronto London Auckland Sydney

Copyright © 1963, 1964, 1965 by the Register and Tribune Syndicate, Inc. Copyright © 1966 by Scholastic Magazines, Inc. This edition is published by Scholastic Book Services, a division of Scholastic Magazines, Inc., by arrangement with the Register and Tribune Syndicate, Inc.

5th printing .... March 1971

Printed in the U.S.A.

THE BIG DIPPER

THE GAME IS
IN THE BAG

THE TWENTIETH SENTRY

"Do you like my company?"
"I don't know—what company are you with?"

COUNTERPART

THE WORST SPELL OF WEATHER WE'VE HAD IN A LONG TIME

ASTER KNOT

♪ ◎N TOP OF OLD
SMOKEY ♫

HE KNEADS THE
DOUGH

CLICK

WATTS GOING
ON

TOEING THE LINE

"**I**'d like to buy a record by the Beatles."
"Single?"
"Yes, but I'm engaged to be married."

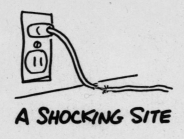

A SHOCKING SITE

A MAN OUTSTANDING IN HIS FIELD

"The doctor told me to drink some lemon juice after a hot bath."

"Did you drink the lemon juice?"

"No, I haven't finished drinking the hot bath yet."

MUTTER OF
PEARL

THE BEE TILLS

NET
RESULTS

ROCK AROUND
THE CLOCK

ODD BAWL

STRETCHING
A HIT

A CATTY
REMARK

CHAIR AND CHAIR
ALIKE

 FALSE HOOD

 A LOT ON HIS MIND

 CONCEITED

"**G**ive me a sentence using the word 'diploma.'"
"Our drain was stopped up, so we called diploma."

FOUR GIVE AND FOUR GET

SHOEING THE CAT

HERMIT

A JEEP'S GATE

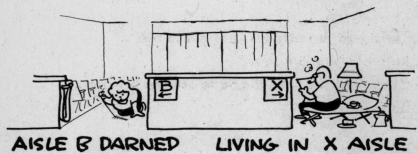

AISLE B DARNED   LIVING IN X AISLE

"**D**id you run across the street to see how old Mrs. Smith is?"
"Yes, and she says it's none of your business how old she is."

BROADCAST

THE HEAT IS
IN TENTS

LISTENING TO AN
UGLY ROOMER

LIGHT ON HIS FEAT

"I made two trips to Europe and I never took a bath."
"You dirty double-crosser!"

HOOTENANNY

STAGE STRUCK

**STORE IN A
COOL PLACE**

**WESTERN
SON SET**

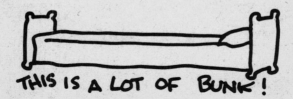

THIS IS A LOT OF BUNK!

SUBTITLE

**A LITTLE DOWN
IN THE MOUTH**

"**W**hat kind of car did you get?"
"I can't remember the name, but it starts with 'T.' "
"Amazing! Most cars use gasoline!"

HE LOOKS
FORBIDDING

READY
TO BLAST
OFF?

LAUNCH MEET

HIDE
AND
ZEKE

DEVIL IN DE SKIES

HOLDING UP A STAGE COACH

SKIRTING THE LAW

THE LAST RESORT

"I'm going to sneeze."

"At whom?"

"At-choo!"

CROCUS

LEGISLATOR

"**I just had my face lifted.**"
"**Who would steal such a thing?**"

TANK'S GIBBON

EWE AND DYE

ROBIN'S SON CREW SO

HANDING HER A LION

"The man who marries my daughter is getting a prize."
"Could I see the prize?"

3 CHAIRS FOR THE RED, WHITE & BLUE.

TANKS FOR EVERYTHING

SHEER DELIGHT

HARE COT

"I have a chance for the baseball team."
"I didn't know they were raffling it off."

WOODEN EWE?

ERASER

CARRYING
CHARGES

SPOT REMOVER

"**W**here is yesterday's newspaper?"
"I wrapped the garbage in it and threw it out."
"Aw, I wanted to see it."
"Wasn't much to look at—just some orange peels and coffee grounds."

THE PIECEMAKERS

LIMBO

SCALING THE FENCE

DRAWN AND QUARTERED

"**C**an you contribute something
to help the Old Ladies' Home?"
"Good grief! Are they out again?"

CROSSBOW

SEASONS' GREETINGS

FANNING THE BATTER

SWITCH
HITTER

SAILS TACKS

A BORING JOB

Hi my
name is

"I have the face of a sixteen-year-old girl."
"Well, you better give it back—you're getting it all wrinkled."

HE DOESN'T
GIVE A
HOOT

A KNIGHT OUT WITH
THE BUOYS

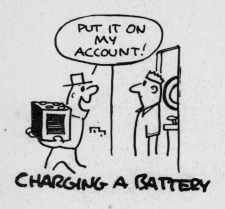

CHARGING A BATTERY

TAKING A TERN
FOR THE WURST

"**A**re the astronauts in?"
"No. They're out to launch."

MINDING HIS
GRAMMAR

TAKING A REIGN CHECK

A KASHMIR SWEATER

SICK CHUTER

CHECKER BORED

HATCHET!

"I've changed my mind."
"Good! I hope this one works."

HARE ON
THE CHEST

A LITTLE MOWER
OF EVERYTHING

TELECAST

PARK IN SPACE

"I swallowed some uranium."
"What happened?"
"I got atomic ache."

ACUTE
TRIANGLE

AUTO
MOBILE

ORGANIZE

HOME
SWEET
HOME

FOUR SAIL

AN OILY BIRD

"**H**ave your eyes ever been checked?"
"No, they've always been plain blue."

I II III IV V VI VII VIII IX X XI XII

A ROMAN RULER

EGGS SPEAR A MINT

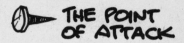
THE POINT OF ATTACK

"How do you like the socks I mended?"
"They're darned good."

GIRLS' NAMES
Rita
Rose
Ruby
Sally
Sarah

ly
am
rel
eba
ethel

RUTHLESS

DE BAIT ON TV

DEHYDRATED

THE CLOCK STRUCK
TWO

"I've proposed to four different men without avail."
"Next time try wearing a veil."

LITTLE RED SCHOOL HOUSE

ADD-A-LESSON

LITTLE SEIZER

"**W**hat's a metaphor?"
"To keep cows in."

AN ELEPHANT CHOKE

ATOM MISER

PICADOR

SQUAW BURY
SHORTCAKE

6'

2'6"

GREW SOME

"Our dog is just like one of the family."
"Which one?"

THIS DOESN'T MAKE CENTS

A LONG LETTER FROM HOME

A HARROWING
EXPERIENCE

CAT 'LYST

YANKERS AWAY

POLICE BEAR WITH US

PARAFIN

"**A** man sold me the Nile River."
"Egypt you."

HOG WASH

A BANQUET

ONE DARNED THING
AFTER ANOTHER

MEAN MICE SHADOW

HAY EWE!

ANOTHER DROP OUT

"**C**ommissar! Commissar! The troops are revolting!"
"Well, you're pretty repulsive yourself!"

RAPPED SODY 'N' BLEW

HOLLER DAZE

"**G**randma fell down a flight of stairs."
"Cellar?"
"No, I think she can be repaired."

EVE'S
DROPPING

LIGHTING A MATCH

JUST DESSERTS

MOON CRATER

HODS AND HENS

CLUCK CLUCK CLUCK

FOWL LANGUAGE

"**H**ow did you pass the geometry test?"
"I knew all the angles."

A FOOT RULE

MANY TANKS!

BUOYS AND GULLS
TOGETHER

"**D**o you like the pogo stick I bought for you."
"Yes, it makes me very hoppy."

HE'S LOOKING OVER
A FOUR LOAF CLEAVER

WATCHING THE SON RISE

KNIGHT BEFORE CHRISTMAS

"The national sport in Spain is bull fighting and in England it's cricket."

"I'd rather be in England."

"Why?"

"It'd be much easier to fight a cricket."

HE CAN'T FIND
HIS MUMMY

A PORPOISE
IN LIFE

A GRIM FURRY TAIL

AN EARLY SETTLER

FILLING STATION

PET AGREED

ICE COLD
POP

A STIRRING
SCENE

PERSUADE

"The doctor examined me for an insurance policy."
"Did he find one?"

BOYCOTT

FRAYED
KNOT

PHOTO FINISH

PARADOX

BAD MITTEN

REST
IN
PIECE

A GRAVE
MISTAKE

"**W**ill you pass the nuts, Professor?"
"Yes, I suppose I will, but I really should flunk them."

FOWL LINE

CHECKING A COUNT

STOCKS AND BONDS

STEP DOTTER

"**W**aiter, bring me a pork chop and make it lean."

"Which way?"